WORLDS OF THE PAST

THE INCAS

Sarita Kendall

new Discovery
B·O·O·K·S
New York

First New Discovery Books edition 1992

Originally published by
HEINEMANN CHILDREN'S REFERENCE
a division of Heinemann Educational Books Ltd
Halley Court, Jordan Hill, Oxford OX2 8EJ

OXFORD LONDON EDINBURGH
MELBOURNE SYDNEY AUCKLAND
MADRID ATHENS BOLOGNA
SINGAPORE IBADAN NAIROBI HARARE
GABORONE KINGSTON PORTSMOUTH NH(USA)

© Heinemann Educational Books Ltd 1991
First published 1991

Designed by Julian Holland Publishing Ltd
Color artwork by Martin Smillie
Picture research by Faith Perkins
Editorial planning by Jackie Gaff

New Discovery Books
Macmillan Publishing Company
866 Third Avenue
New York, NY 10022

Macmillan Publishing Company is part of the
Maxwell Communication Group of Companies.

Printed in Hong Kong

First Edition
10 9 8 7 6 5 4 3 2 1

Library of Congress Cataloging-in-Publication Data
Kendall, Sarita.
      The Incas / Sarita Kendall.
          p.   cm. — (Worlds of the Past)
      Includes index.
      Summary: Surveys the civilization, history, and culture of
the Incas, including studies of their government,
religion, family life, agriculture, and architecture.
      ISBN 0-02-750160-4
      1. Incas — Juvenile literature. [1. Incas. 2. Indians of South
America.] I. Title. II. Series.
F3429.K48   1992
985'.01 — dc20   91 − 513

Photographic acknowledgments
The author and publisher wish to acknowledge, with
thanks, the following photographic sources:
a = above, *b* = below, *c* = center, *l* = left, *r* = right
Cover: *a* and *bl* Tony and Marion Morrison; *br* Sarita
Kendall. Cusichaca Trust pp7*a*, 30*b*, 35*c*, 35*b*, 36; Robert
Francis p43; Robert Harding p17*b*; Horniman Museum/
photograph B Brandon p8; Hulton Collection p56*a*; Ann
Kendall pp4*a* and *b*, 37*c*, 41, 45, 47*b*, 54*b*, 55; Sarita
Kendall pp6, 12, 15, 16, 19*b*, 22*a*, 22*b*, 24, 25, 26*a*, 27, 29,
31, 32*b* 33, 34, 37*a*, 39*a*, 39*c*, 40, 42*a* and *b*, 48*b*, 49*a*, 52,
53*a*, 57, 59*a* and *b*; Loren McIntyre p50; Tony and Marion
Morrison pp1, 9, 10*a* and *b*, 11, 14, 17*a*, 18, 19*a*, 21*b*, 23,
26*b*, 28*c* and *b*, 30*a*, 32*a*, 35*a*, 38*c*, 39*b*, 44*l* and *r*, 46*a*, 48*a*,
51, 53*b*, 54*a*, 56*b*, 61; Timothy Ross p58*a* and *b*; Bruce
Sampson pp7*c*, 20, 38*b*, 49*c*; Science Photo Library 21*a*
The publishers have made every effort to trace the
copyright holders but if they have inadvertently
overlooked any, they will be pleased to make the
necessary arrangement at the first opportunity.

Note to the reader
In this book there are some words in the text which are printed in **bold** type. This shows that the word is listed in
the glossary on page 62. The glossary gives a brief explanation of words which may be new to you.

Contents

Who were the Incas?

About 800 years ago a group of people called the Incas settled in the Cuzco Valley, high up in the Andes Mountains of South America. Exactly where they came from, who they were, and when they reached Cuzco no one really knows.

By the 1400s the Incas had conquered neighboring peoples and had established a strong, well-run state around Cuzco. Over the next 100 years, Inca rulers led their armies along the slopes of the Andes, through deep forested gorges and into the desert area near the coast of the Pacific Ocean. Their empire stretched more than 2,170 miles (3,500 km) from north to south. The Incas governed over six million people in this huge territory. They were strong rulers, making sure that all the people knew their own place in Inca society, and what their rights and duties were.

When the Spaniards arrived in what is now Peru, they marveled at Inca cities, roads, and fortresses. Above all they were dazzled by the amount of gold jewelry and decoration they saw. Only two years after they marched into the Andean valleys, a determined group of gold-greedy Spanish adventurers had murdered the Inca ruler and prepared to conquer the empire.

△ This big jar was used for carrying liquids such as maize beer, or chicha. It is called an aryballus and jars of this shape were found only in the Inca empire. By passing a rope through the handles, the jar could be hoisted onto somebody's back. These jars were usually decorated with geometric designs on the side facing outward.

◁ As the Inca empire grew, cities were built in newly conquered areas. Tambo Colorado was an important administrative center on the coast, south of modern Lima. These ruins of the city show Inca style alcoves or niches built into the adobe walls. And there are still signs of the red and white painted decoration.

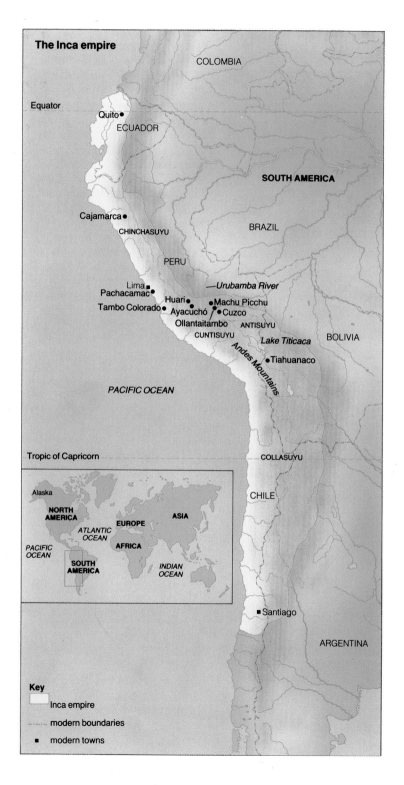

The Inca empire

COLOMBIA

Equator

Quito●
ECUADOR

SOUTH AMERICA

Cajamarca●

CHINCHASUYU

BRAZIL

PERU

Lima■
Pachacamac●
Huari●
Tambo Colorado●
Ayacuchó● ●Machu Picchu
●Cuzco
Ollantaitambo
CUNTISUYU
ANTISUYU

—Urubamba River

Lake Titicaca
BOLIVIA
●Tiahuanaco

PACIFIC OCEAN

Andes Mountains

Tropic of Capricorn

COLLASUYU

CHILE

Alaska
NORTH
AMERICA
ATLANTIC
OCEAN
EUROPE
ASIA
PACIFIC
OCEAN
AFRICA
SOUTH
AMERICA
INDIAN
OCEAN

■Santiago

ARGENTINA

Key

☐ Inca empire

---- modern boundaries

■ modern towns

◁ The Incas called their empire Tahuantinsuyu, "The Land of the Four Quarters." It was divided into Chinchasuyu, the northwest area, Collasuyu, the southeast area, Antisuyu, the northeast area, and Cuntisuyu, the southwest area. Much of the empire was over 9,843 feet (3,000 m) high, with snow peaks 19,685 feet (6,000 m). Icy winds blow across the upland plateaus, and from June to August the weather is very dry. The Incas built canals to irrigate their crops of maize, grains, and potatoes which were grown on hillside terraces in the valleys. On the desert coast, people survived in fertile oases where rivers watered the dry ground.

By 1532, when the Spaniards invaded, the Tahuantinsuyu covered an area nearly twice the size of Spain and about equal to Texas and New Mexico combined.

How we know about the Incas

The story of the Incas has to be pieced together from different kinds of evidence. In some cities like Pisac and Machu Picchu, the ruins show us how the Incas planned and built their towns. Spanish **chroniclers,** or historians, also wrote accounts of the last days of the Inca empire.

Archaeologists have collected evidence to show how the Incas and other people lived in the past. The tools, cloth, and pottery found by them are in museums. Often Inca towns and roads are covered with earth or hidden by modern buildings. So the archaeologists dig into the ground to discover what the town was like and what can be learned about the Incas from the objects they left behind. Great care must be taken when **excavating**, or digging. Somebody draws or photographs each object to show exactly where it is found. Robbers destroy this

▽ On a cold drizzly morning in 1911, the American explorer Hiram Bingham climbed with his guide through dense jungle up to some terraces above the Urubamba River. Suddenly he found himself among ruined houses of the finest Inca stonework, which were half-hidden by tangled vines and moss. Gradually, as the vegetation was cleared away, a whole Inca city was discovered. Hiram Bingham believed the city was Vilcabamba, where the last Incas hid from the Spaniards, but experts now agree that this lay farther into the jungle, at Espiritu Pampa. Bingham had discovered the city of Machu Picchu.

◁ Sometimes studying how people lived in the past can help us today. For instance, if irrigation canals are found, they can be rebuilt to help water crops grown today. Also, if there is evidence that a crop once grew well in an area where it is no longer grown, people might try to grow it again.

kind of evidence when they dig for gold.

Some materials last much longer than others. Houses built by the Incas in the highland areas were often made of stone. These lasted much longer than sun-dried mud walls. However, mud walls were well preserved by the dry coastal desert climate. Looking at pottery is one of the best ways of learning about how people lived. It keeps well, and nearly everyone in the Inca empire used pottery. Because of this, different shapes and designs can easily be recognized.

One clue to the existence of Inca sites may be the sight of unusual bumps on a hillside. Sometimes these have turned out to be old farm terraces, or half-buried stone slabs which had a religious purpose. These mounds can be detected by taking photographs of the land from an airplane or by walking over the mountain trails in the Andes.

In many places the people of the Andes still keep some of the old Inca customs. They speak **Quechua**, a language which was used throughout the Inca empire.

▽ Few Inca sites have been properly excavated. Nowadays historians, geographers, botanists, and other scientists, as well as the archaeologists, take part in the study of a site.

Clues from the past

The origin of the Inca civilization goes back thousands of years to the time when people first crossed from Asia to Alaska and began moving southward through the Americas. Stone tools found near Ayacucho show that traveling people called nomads, who lived by hunting animals, had arrived in the Andes by 12,000 B.C. Some archaeologists believe these nomads may have been there as early as 20,000 B.C.

As people learned how to grow crops, groups of them gave up their nomadic life and settled in one place. By 2000 B.C., maize, beans, cotton, and some root crops such as potatoes were being grown, and people had begun to make pottery. Small villages became towns, and some places had special buildings such as temples. The Chavín people decorated buildings with stone carvings, that showed snakes, birds, and jaguars.

From about 2,000 years ago several states began to develop on the coast. The best-known people were the Nazca in the south and the Mochica in the north. Mochica pots are painted with wonderful details of everyday life, which show that many Inca customs go back to this period.

△ The Mochica made lifelike pots of human faces, animals, and other figures. They also painted fishing, weaving, and other everyday activities on their pots. Enormous Mochica pyramids built of adobe bricks have been found in the northern coastal desert.

B.C. and A.D.
Each year has a number. These numbers, or dates, record when things happen. Dates are measured from the year when Jesus Christ was born. Any date before the birth of Christ is called B.C. The date is written with the letter after the number (2000 B.C.). Remember that 1000 B.C. is more recent than 2000 B.C. Dates since the birth of Christ have the letters A.D. They stand for *Anno Domini*. These Latin words mean "in the year of the Lord." So A.D. 1 means "in the first year of the life of Christ, the Lord." The letters A.D. always come before the date.

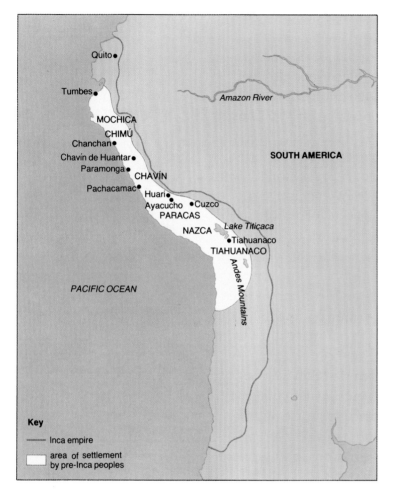

◁ The first people to live in the central Andes came from the north. Fine temples at Chavín de Huantar were among the earliest to be built. Then, about the time of the birth of Christ, the Nazca and Mochica states grew up. By about A.D. 1000 the Tianuanaco and Huari people dominated most of the central-south Andes. The Chimú had built a huge city in the northern desert at Chanchan when the Incas began to extend their empire.

△ From about 700 B.C. people in the Andes region began to weave fine tapestries and cloth. The textiles of Paracas, on the southern coast, combined intricate animal and human figures embroidered on dark backgrounds. About 200 different colors made from natural dyes have been identified. The weaving techniques used by the Incas were known as Paracas.

In the highlands, the great Tiahuanaco religious center near Lake Titicaca confirms that there were skilled stonemasons long before the Incas. The people of Tiahuanaco seem to have had close links with the Huari empire, which had its capital in the Ayacucho region. This empire, though never as big as the **Tahuantinsuyu**, was similar in some ways. Roads and towns were built to administer conquered territories. No one knows why the Huari empire collapsed around A.D. 1000, but the Andean peoples had no central government from that time until the Incas began to build their empire.

Evidence in words and pictures

The Incas had no written language but they used other ways of keeping records and passing on information. One way was to repeat stories, songs, and poems again and again so they would not be forgotten. Inca rulers often chose talented people to make up story-songs that told of great deeds. These ballads were recited on special occasions. Statistics were carefully recorded on long strands of knotted strings called **quipus**. Each knot represented a number, according to how the knot was tied and where it came on the string. Quipus were used by a **quipucamayoc** to count the population, to keep information on military campaigns, and for recording amounts of farm products.

Much of what we know about the Incas comes from letters, reports, and histories written by Spanish soldiers and priests who came to conquer and convert. However a few authors recorded Inca civilization in detail: Pedro Cieza de León who traveled for 17 years along the Inca roads, first as a young soldier, later as a historian; Martín de Murua, a traveling preacher or friar living in the Andes soon after the conquest; and Father Bernabé Cobo, a priest and historian who studied the Incas.

△ This picture of Huaman Poma comes from his famous picture history that was discovered in a Copenhagen library early in this century. Today it gives us a clear idea of Inca clothes and customs.

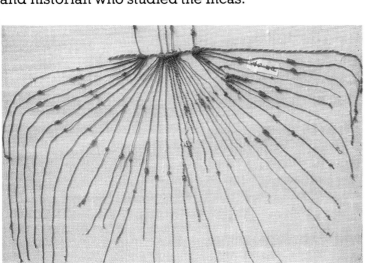

◁ The quipu had one main cord with colored cotton or wool threads hanging from it. Cieza de León said the quipus were so exact that not even a pair of sandals went unrecorded. The knots could also help trained quipu keepers, or quipucamayocs, recall past events.

Some writers described the Incas as tyrants and savages, but they did not mention the Spaniards' cruelty and injustice toward the conquered people. One chieftain called Huaman Poma wrote a picture history for the king of Spain, telling him of the suffering of his people. Garcilaso de la Vega, the son of an Inca princess, was influenced by the Inca point of view, though he began his Royal Commentaries long after leaving home to live in Spain.

◁ Huaman Poma's drawing shows a quipucamayoc, with a kind of abacus for adding on the left. Unfortunately the art of "reading" the quipu was lost after the Incas were conquered.

Building an empire

The Incas did not calculate long periods of time as we do. Instead they thought in terms of 1,000-year cycles. This means there are no exact dates for the earlier Inca reigns, though historians agree on the names of the rulers.

The historian John Rowe worked out that if there were twelve rulers up to 1532, the Inca dynasty could not have been founded before A.D. 1200. This fits archaeological evidence from pre-Inca and Inca sites. The first Inca, Manco Capac, was a mysterious figure. He claimed the sun was his father, and one legend tells how he appeared from the mouth of a cave wearing a shining cloak.

The first eight Inca rulers gradually built a small, strong state with the city of Cuzco as its center. The ninth ruler, Pachacuti Inca Yupanqui, won a great victory against the Chanca people and began the long-distance military campaigns that led to the growth of the Inca empire. Pachacuti first marched to the lower Urubamba Valley, extending his northern frontier beyond the gorge where the city of Machu Picchu was later built. Then he led an army south

△ The Incas did not conquer just to grow richer. With their rule came a more, settled way of life and new skills. To help teach Inca customs, or to deal with rebellious tribes, groups of skilled people called mitimaes were transferred from one part of the empire to another. Some were sent to the southeastern valleys (*above*) to grow tropical crops. Others lived in newly conquered areas near Quito. Some went from the high Andes to bring order to the restless tribes around Lake Titicaca.

The Inca dynasty	
Manco Capac	about 1200
Sinchi Roca	
Lloque Yupanqui	
Mayta Capac	
Capac Yupanqui	
Inca Roca	
Yahuar Huacae	about 1400
Viracocha Inca	
Pachacuti Inca Yupanqui	1438–1471
Topa Inca Yupanqui	1471–1493
Huayna Capac	1493–1525
Huáscar	1525–1532
Atahuallpa	1532–1533
After the Spanish conquest, the Inca rulers had no real power.	

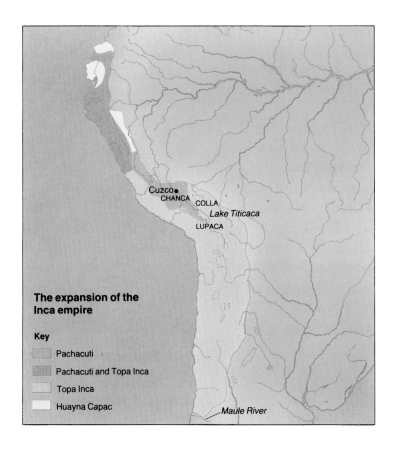

The expansion of the
Inca empire

Key

Pachacuti

Pachacuti and Topa Inca

Topa Inca

Huayna Capac

Cuzco
CHANCA
COLLA
Lake Titicaca
LUPACA

Maule River

◁ The Inca empire began to grow with Pachacuti's victory over the Chanca people, northwest of Cuzco. He also conquered the Colla and Lupaca tribes around Lake Titicaca, though they rebelled later. Topa Inca won most of the northern Andes and desert coast, then set the southern boundary of the empire at the Maule River in present day Chile. Huayna Capac added new lands in the north, extending Inca rule as far as today's boundary between Colombia and Ecuador.

across the high plains to fight the Colla and Lupaca tribes.

Pachacuti was a brilliant general and an extraordinary ruler. He rebuilt Cuzco and reorganized the government in order to control the growing empire, while his son, Topa Inca Yupanqui, swept northward as far as the city of Quito. Many tribes chose to join the Incas as allies, rather than fight the Inca army. Doubling back along the coast, Topa Inca defeated the powerful Chimu people.

The Incas imposed their religion, their laws, and the Quechua language throughout the empire, but they also respected local traditions. Conquered chiefs often remained in power, though their sons were sent to Cuzco as hostages to learn Inca ways.

The Sapa Inca

Viracocha Inca, who was the eighth ruler, used the title of Sapa Inca, meaning "Unique Inca." From then on all the rulers were known as the Sapa Inca, though they were also called Powerful Lord and Son of the Sun. Inca rulers were thought to be the sun's representative on earth. This meant that their power was like that of a god. The chroniclers said that even great chiefs trembled in the Sapa Inca's presence. Visitors took off their sandals and approached him backward, bowing low to show respect.

At the Inca's court his relatives occupied important positions and had special rights. There were also the personal servants, the **yanacona**, who looked after the Sapa Inca as well as a large bodyguard of warriors. All the pomp and grandeur that surrounded the Sapa Inca made him seem far above his people. Because it helped to make ordinary people fear their ruler, he was obeyed without question.

The Incas' heir

Stories about the Incas' arrival in Cuzco usually tell of a family of eight, but sometimes six, brothers and sisters, including Manco Capac. The first Inca ruler married his sister, Mama Ocllo, who was believed to be the daughter of the moon. From that time, the Sapa Inca usually followed the custom of marrying one of his sisters. She became his principal wife when he was crowned, and she was called the **Coya**. Although the ruler might have many other wives and children, only his sons by the Coya were supposed to inherit the empire.

The eldest son did not always become Sapa Inca. According to the writer Martín de Murua, if one of the other sons seemed more astute and capable of war and government, that son would become the next ruler.

△ The Sapa Inca had many advisers, including his own relatives and other nobles. He sat on a platform or throne to receive generals, ambassadors, and officials from all corners of the Tahuantinsuyu.

The Inca and the Incas
The word *Inca* really refers to the original Inca tribe and the Inca ruler, but members of the royal family were also called Incas. After the Spanish conquest, writers often described all the people of the empire as Incas.

How the Inca lived

The Sapa Inca and the Coya lived in separate palaces. The palaces were very luxurious, with fine hangings and gold decoration. Two great, well-guarded entrances led into patios or courtyards. Beyond the patios was the living area. Martín de Murua said there were secret underground passages joining the two palaces, so that the Sapa Inca could visit the Coya. Gardens, baths, and temples were laid out within the walls, and tame birds flew into the Coya's hand, according to Garcilaso de la Vega. The finest trees, the sweetest smelling herbs, and the most beautiful flowers were grown in the palace gardens. These gardens were full of delights such as butterflies made of gold, and "fields" of corn made of silver stalks and golden ears.

▽ Every Sapa Inca built his own palace in Cuzco, and decorated it as grandly as he pleased. He also kept other palaces or country houses where he could rest on his journeys through the empire. This palace, overlooking the Urubamba River, was thought to have been built by the eighth Inca, Viracocha. It is surrounded by farm terraces, so the Sapa Inca's family was always well supplied with food.

Government and society

Inca society was strictly organized. The highest social rank was that of the Sapa Inca and his family. Sometimes people from other tribes were also given the privilege of becoming Inca nobles, though they never equaled the royal family's social position. When the empire was expanding, many of these unrelated nobles were given important jobs in the new provinces. Judges, engineers, and quipucamayocs were all considered important people in the ruling of the empire.

The Sapa Inca had a council of four **apus**, each of whom was responsible for one of the **suyus**, the four quarters of the empire. The apus were usually related to the Sapa Inca. So, too, were the governors who lived in provincial capitals. Below the governors came local rulers, or **curacas**, and then the district headman, or **camayoc**. These local leaders were responsible for governing a certain number of households and for enforcing Inca laws.

▽ The taxpayer often had to serve up to five years' labor in the army, the mines, or the public works force. This time was called a mita. In many Andean communities people also worked together on houses or repairing local tracks. This custom, called minga, still exists in villages north of Quito and elsewhere.

◁ Father Cobo described the weaving and embroidery skills of the Incas. The clothes of high-ranking nobles were decorated with red, gold, green, blue, and yellow feathers from jungle birds. The feathers were sewn into the fine cloth to make brightly colored patterns.

Many Inca laws were concerned with land, **tribute,** and labor. The idea was that people should have to work hard, then they would be well fed and clothed, but they would not own many possessions. There were also moral laws, with punishments for lying, drunkenness, and murder. These punishments were harsh, including whipping and even death. Inca nobles, however, were dealt with much less severely if they broke these laws.

Working taxes

Inspectors visited the provinces to decide on the quantity of food and goods each area should send in to the capital as tribute to the Sapa Inca. Most taxpayers, who were men over 25 years old, paid their tribute by working on the land. Farming families often worked together to pay their tribute. Not a single village of the highlands or the plains failed to pay the tribute levied on it, according to Cieza de León. Nobles, officers, curacas, and women did not pay taxes.

△ To show their high rank the Sapa Inca and his nobles wore big earplugs. The Spaniards nicknamed them *orejones* — big ears! The earplugs could be as much as 1.95 inches (5 cm) across and they were often made of gold.

Clothes and appearance

Clothes, especially headdresses, were a guide to a person's rank in Inca society. They also showed which part of the empire somebody came from. The quality of the cloth, the colors, the designs, and the jewelry varied a great deal, but the basic style of dress did not.

In the highland areas, fine woolen cloth was woven from the coats of animals related to the llama, the **alpaca,** or the **vicuña.** People who lived in the hotter coastal areas wore cotton. More people began to wear cotton after roads were built and it was easier to trade.

Women wore full-length, straight, sleeveless dresses. The dress was belted with a broad woven sash wound several times around the waist. Over their shoulders, they wore long cloaks, fastened in front with gold, silver, or bronze pins called *tupus*. A pair of sandals completed the outfit. Women kept their hair long and parted it in the middle. They tied back their hair with headbands, or sometimes they braided it.

Men wore short, loose tunics with holes for the head and arms. A man's cloak was usually quite short, but there were longer, full cloaks, too. The cloak was knotted on the shoulder or over the chest. Sandals for both sexes were made by the men out of llama leather, wool, and a fiber from the prickly aloe plant.

In Huaman Poma's drawings the Inca ruler often has squares and other geometric designs woven into a band around the middle of his tunic. For special occasions the tunic would be decorated all over in the richest colors. Bright colors, patterned borders, and complicated designs showed high status.

Royal women's clothes were also more decorative than the ordinary person's. Women wore a folded cloth pinned onto their hair, which hung down over their shoulders. Cieza de León said that the clothes of

△ The Coya and the Sapa Inca bathed often, and there were sunken baths with hot and cold water in the royal palaces. Here the Coya washes and combs her hair, helped by the royal princesses, the nustas. The combs were made of long thorns, bound together onto a piece of wood.

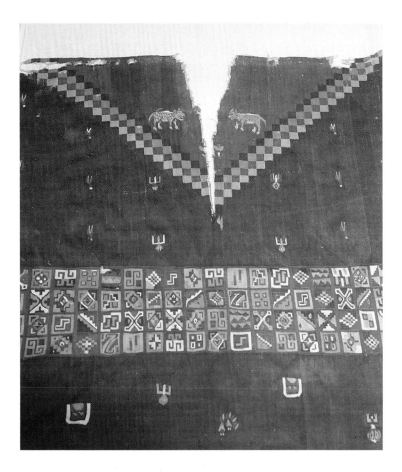

◁ Only a few clothes have survived in the highlands because of the damp climate. This tunic would have been worn by a man of high rank in Inca society.

the women of Cuzco were the best and the finest to be seen. Spanish historians were impressed by how often the Inca and the Coya changed their clothes. Martín de Murua said that the Sapa Inca never wore the same tunic twice.

The men's headdresses and jewelry were grander and more varied than the women's. Nobles wore broad gold armbands, and small gold masks were sometimes sewn on the tunic and the sandals.

Historians mentioned the many different headbands, which identified each person's tribe. The tradition has survived. Highlanders today can usually tell which village somebody comes from by the style of his or her hat.

△ The women in Otavalo, north of Quito, still wear clothes very like those of Inca women. Only the embroidered blouse is of modern design. The necklaces of an Inca woman would have been made of shell or bone.

19

The Inca gods

Viracocha was the Incas' god of creation. He was believed to have created the sun and the moon, the stars, the animals, the sea, and the earth, as well as men and women. The first Spanish soldiers to go to Cuzco said they saw a statue of Viracocha in the form of a boy. He was not usually worshiped by ordinary people and Inca prayers quoted by the Spaniards refer to him as an invisible god, high in the heavens.

Inti, the sun, the father of the Incas, was the most important god in official Inca religion. Farmers in the cold highlands depended on the sun for warmth to ripen their crops. Many other Andean peoples as well as the Incas were sun worshipers. Mama Quilla, mother moon, was the sun's wife and the mother of the Incas. Just as the Sapa Inca represented the sun on earth, the Coya represented the moon.

The Inca gods
Viracocha: the god of creation.

Inti: the sun, father of the Inca dynasty. Powerful but kind and life-giving.

Illapa: the god of rain, thunder, and lightning. He was the messenger of Inti.

Mama Quilla: mother moon, mother of the Incas. She was important for calculating the months of the year.

The stars: children of the sun and moon. These included Venus, the Pleiades, and Lyra. Groups of stars looked after certain things on earth. For example, the Pleiades protected plant seeds.

Pacha Mama: mother earth. She was the goddess who looked after the fields and everything in the ground. She was often represented by a slab of stone in a field.

Mama Cocha: mother of the lakes. Fishermen along the coast worshiped her as mother of the sea.

◁ Many Andean people worshiped the sun. At Tiahuanaco a stone gateway is known as the Gateway of the Sun.

◁ The Pleiades were, and still are, one of the most important groups of stars to the Andean peoples because they looked after farming communities and seeds.

In the harsh Andean environment, earth tremors, volcanic eruptions, sudden hailstorms, and many other natural disasters are common. It is easy to understand why people believed that there was a link between the gods' actions and their own survival. The gods had to be kept happy, otherwise they might punish people by sending a drought or other bad luck.

When the Incas conquered new areas, they let people keep their idols and continue worshiping their own gods, as long as the sun religion came first. The Incas themselves sometimes acknowledged well-known gods in other regions. They spoke to the god who could be contacted through a holy place, an **oracle**, at Pachacamac on the coast. They even built a sun temple beside the oracle.

△ Pacha Mama stones or boulders are found in fields farmed during Inca times. People may still make offerings to the goddess before starting to work on the land.

Temples and shrines

Throughout the Andes, people worshiped and made offerings to mountains, streams, or animals. These holy places or objects were known as **huacas**. The Incas prayed at 328 huacas in the area around Cuzco, according to the writer Bernabé Cobo. One of these was the hilltop of Huanacauri, near Cuzco. Other huacas included temples, tombs, stones, and the sites of battles.

These huacas were grouped along imaginary lines, or **ceques,** which led out from Cuzco. Father Cobo said family groups looked after certain ceques. Experts now believe the ceque system was an important part of Inca astronomy.

Gods and huacas often had to be worshiped at particular times or when people were doing certain tasks. For example, women sowing seeds would pray to Pacha Mama and pour some maize beer on the ground. Travelers might add a stone to a pile of rocks, an **apacita**, on a mountain pass, asking the gods for a safe journey. Martín de Murua said it was common to bow the head and raise the arms while praying aloud. People often carried lucky charms or **amulets** for protection.

△ At Tambo Machay, which was on one of the ceque lines, Father Cobo tells us there were three huacas. Sacrifices were made in the main house, and both the fountain and the spring were considered holy places. Tambo Machay itself was probably a hunting lodge used by Inca royalty.

◁ Gods were kept satisfied with offerings of coca leaves, maize, and chicha. Gold objects, feathers, and shells have also been found at huaca sites. Miners made special sacrifices of llamas so that the earth, the goddess Pacha Mama, would yield them her riches. This ceremony is still carried out today. At this mine in Bolivia, coca leaves and liquor are scattered over the llamas and their blood is splashed around the tunnel. The miners have a feast to honor the goddess.

Worshiping the huacas was a simple, direct way of bargaining with the gods. The Incas also had much more elaborate religious customs. They built magnificent temples in Cuzco and other cities. These temples were looked after by priests who heard people's confessions, made sacrifices to the gods, and listened to the oracles. The head priest, **uillac uma**, was one of the most important people in the empire. He was also a close relative of the Sapa Inca.

Young women and girls were chosen to serve in the temples in Cuzco. Some of these women, called **aclla,** or chosen, became priestesses. They lived in special houses or convents, called **acllahuasi**, near the temples, where they wove very fine cloth and prepared ceremonial food in honor of the sun-god.

The temples contained statues and images of the gods and goddesses. The royal family worshiped in the temples, but the people took part in open-air ceremonies in the city center. Every day a llama was killed as a sacrifice to the gods and food was offered to the sun, the god of gods.

▽ Coricancha, the sun temple in Cuzco, was richly decorated with gold. The curved wall of tightly fitting masonry supported the temple, which stood at the center of the ceque lines radiating from Cuzco. In the seventeenth century the Spaniards built a church on the same site, using some of the Inca stonework. Excavations inside the church have been carried out recently.

The Inca calendar

Historians have never been sure how much astronomy the Incas understood. Some writers spoke of an eight-day week. Huaman Poma wrote of three ten-day weeks making up a month. This meant several days had to be added to make a year of 365 days if it was calculated by the sun, a **solar** year.

Inca astronomers, often the priests, watched the position of the sun, the moon, and Venus. One historian studied a collection of quipus which had probably been used for astronomical records and decided that the Incas knew exactly how some of the planets revolved. They seem to have measured the sun's movements in relation to stone towers built on the hills east and west of Cuzco. According to the writer Garcilaso de la Vega, there were four towers on each horizon, two tall and two shorter ones. However, no one has found any remains of them. The astronomer-priests may have kept their calculations from the Spaniards, to protect their religious beliefs.

▽ The sun temples at Machu Picchu and Pisac were also astronomical observatories. The *Inti huatana*, meaning "the post to which the sun is tied," probably had a special astronomical, as well as religious, importance.

Any unusual events, such as eclipses of the sun or moon, and falling stars, were considered to be bad omens. So were some everyday things, like an owl hooting. Dreams were thought to bring warnings. The people offered sacrifices before they made important decisions, so that the gods would give them good advice.

△ Flutes and drums were, and still are, played all through the Andes. The quena was a piece of bamboo with finger stops, while panpipes (*above*) were made of several different lengths of bamboo tied together. At festivals, the dancers dressed up in gorgeous costumes. They danced special dances, telling about warriors' lives or farmers' lives. Sometimes the dancers asked for victory in battle or for rain to make the crops grow. Drums were played at these dances.

Festivals and ceremonies

The Inca calendar year was full of festivals and ceremonies marking different aspects of life, especially events in the farming cycle.

Inti raimi: the feast of the sun, June. Great sacrifices, including children, were offered to the sun.

Chahua huarquiz: the plowing month, July.

Yapaquiz: the sowing month, August. A thousand guinea pigs were sacrificed when the first maize was sown in a holy field.

Coya raimi: the feast of the coya, September. Cuzco was purified during the Situa festival; afterward, people smeared maize porridge on their faces.

Uma raimi: the feast of rain, October. People prayed for the rain.

Ayamarca raimi: the feast of the dead, November. The dead were taken out of their tombs to be paraded in the streets and honored.

Capac raimi: the supreme feast, December. The puberty ceremonies, called Huarochico, began at this time.

Camay quilla: the small ripening, January. Huarochico continued with wrestling and mock battles.

Hatun pucuy: the great ripening, February. Twenty guinea pigs and twenty loads of firewood were offered to the sun for the crops.

Pacha pucuy: the earth ripening, March.

Ayrihua: the harvesting, April. A llama was taught to eat coca and drink chicha. It was dressed up and took part in ceremonies in Cuzco.

Aymoray quilla: the harvest festival. There was feasting and dancing as the harvest was safely gathered.

The Inca months did not begin and end at the same time as calendar months do now. For example, Inti raimi ran from late June to late July.

Medicine and healing

The Incas believed that illness was sent by the gods as a punishment, or that it was the result of evil magic. So when illness struck, sacrifices must be offered to the gods. If magic had caused the illness, then the cure had to be magical, too.

Every year disease and evil were banished from Cuzco during the Situa festival when warriors ran from the city center toward the four quarters of the empire. The Incas believed that this ceremony would sweep sickness away. Garcilaso de la Vega said people came out of their houses at this time and shook their clothing, then they bathed. The feasting lasted several days and priests examined the lungs of sacrificial llamas to find out whether the coming year would be a good one.

The Incas knew a great deal about herbal medicine and were also skilled in surgery. The Collahuayna tribe was well known for expert knowledge of plants. Many of their remedies are still used in the countryside around Lake Titicaca.

Cieza de León praised the molle tree for its wonderful qualities. The bark, boiled in water, cured swellings and healed wounds; the twigs were good

△ The coca plant was highly valued by the Incas. It was offered to the gods in religious ceremonies. Chewing the leaves helped take away tiredness and hunger, while coca tea was used for stomach illness. Coca leaves are still chewed in the Andes, and the cocaine extracted from them is important in eye operations.

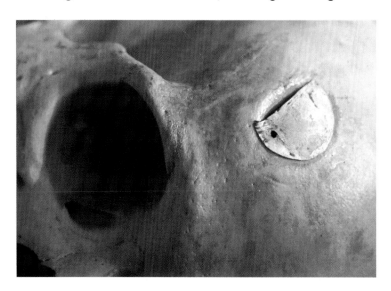

◁ Inca surgeons performed complicated operations. One operation, called trepanning, involved cutting away part of the skull to relieve pressure on the brain. The opening was later covered by a silver plate. The head wounds that made the operation necessary were probably caused in battle. Archaeologists know many patients survived from the number of healed skulls found in graves.

for cleaning teeth and keeping the gums healthy; the berries made an excellent syrup. Cinchona bark reduced fever, and tobacco powder was sniffed to clear the head. Western doctors are realizing more and more that herbal medicines often work. For instance, quinine is a medicine which they use to cure fever. It is made from the bark of the cinchona tree.

Death and burial

When someone died, the relatives dressed in black and women cut their hair. There was a funeral feast with slow dancing. The body was usually placed in a sitting position and wrapped up in fine clothes. The Incas believed life continued after death and that the person who had died would need everyday things, such as pottery, baskets, and food. They buried these objects in the tomb with the body. Sometimes an Inca ruler's wives and servants were buried with him. If archaeologists find weapons in a tomb, they know the person was a warrior. During the November festival of the dead, the wrapped bodies, or mummies, were paraded for special ceremonies.

◁ Many people were buried in tombs made in rocks or caves. Usually there was a small door which was blocked up at the time of burial. On the coast, people were buried underground. Offerings of food and chicha were brought to the graves regularly to please the dead members of the family. In some parts of the Andes, people still keep the custom of visiting family graves in November.

Family life

The Spanish writers were more interested in government than in the family life of the Incas. Bernabe Cobo was one of the few chroniclers to describe people's lives, including their customs and ceremonies, in detail.

Unless they belonged to the royal family, children had no chance to study or play. They had to work with their families. Girls aged about ten might be chosen to join the acllahuasi, the house of the chosen women, in the provincial capital. They were taught weaving, cooking, and religion and went to Cuzco for the sun festival when they were 13 or 14 years old. Some young women were chosen to serve the Sapa Inca, while others dedicated their lives to the sun-god.

Coming of age

Both boys and girls were given their adult names when they reached puberty. A girl's coming-of-age celebration was called the **quicochico** ceremony.

△◁ Babies were wrapped up tightly and tied into a wooden cradle which could be slung on their mother's backs. Andean women still carry their babies on their backs, but nowadays the babies are in a shawl. When a child was nearly two, he or she would be named at a haircutting ceremony, the Rutuchico. Relatives and friends cut a lock of the baby's hair and presented a gift, as they still do nowadays.

After her first menstruation, she fasted for three days, then washed and dressed in new clothes. At the celebration that followed, she was given her new name.

The boys' **huarochico** ceremony was a more public occasion than the girls' celebration. It was linked to the summer solstice festival. The boys' strength, discipline, and other abilities were tested. Sons of the Sapa Inca and the Cuzco nobles made offerings at the Huanacauri shrine and were taken to the temple of the sun. They wore special clothing, visited other religious shrines, and ran races. All this lasted for several weeks. Finally, the Sapa Inca presented the boys with loincloths and gold earplugs. There was a great feast and the boys received weapons and other presents from their families. For ordinary people in the provinces, the ceremony was much simpler.

Marriage

A young woman normally married before she was 20 years old, and a young man when he was 25. Ordinary people were not allowed to marry close relatives, though they had to choose somebody in their community. Some chroniclers say all the young people lined up face-to-face in the town's main square, and had to marry whoever was opposite in the line. It seems more likely that partners had chosen each other in advance.

The bride and groom were married by the Sapa Inca, or, in the provinces, by an Inca official. Later, at home, the bride's father formally gave her to her husband, who fitted a sandal on her right foot. Then the families moved on to the new husband's house, where the bride gave him cloth she had woven. Only when all the formalities were over, could the drinking, feasting, and dancing begin.

▽ The sons of nobles and government officials went to the house of teaching, the yachahuasi, in Cuzco. They learned about Inca society, government, religion, and engineering, as well as quipus and military matters. Other children worked with their parents, the boys looking after the animals and trapping birds, and the girls taking care of babies and doing household chores. Even old people helped with lighter duties in the house.

Living on the land

Long before the Inca conquest, Andean people were organized into groups of related families called **ayllus**. Land belonged to the ayllu as a whole, not to each family.

The Incas shared farmland among the Sapa Inca, the sun and other gods, and the community. The amount of land assigned to the Inca and the priests probably varied according to the fertility of the soil and the size of the population. All land was owned by the state, and the people were given the right to farm certain areas. Inca administrators followed local traditions on land division, although they occasionally rewarded people for special services to the state with land grants. The local chief also continued to distribute ayllu land in accordance with each family's needs.

Most ordinary people in the Inca empire were farmers. If they lived high on the mountain slopes where there were winter frosts, they grew potatoes and kept animals. In the warmer sheltered valleys, such as the Urubamba, maize was cultivated, and lower down still there were fruits, peppers, cocoa, and peanuts. More than 40 different plants were grown in the Andean region before the Spaniards

△ The empire needed a steady food supply, including the produce for the royal family, the priests, and all the people working for the state.

Irrigation was essential to food production in the desert areas, and it improved harvests in the highlands. Although there were irrigation canals before Inca times, the Incas built far bigger and better systems. Mountain streams were diverted along new stone channels that curved around hillsides, and rivers were straightened.

◁ In some places the Incas' irrigation systems are still used. In other places evidence remains of rivers that were straightened. Here in the upper Cusichaca Valley a local river was canalized by the Incas so they could grow potatoes.

◁ The Incas increased the amount of flat land which could be used for farming by building terraces on the hillsides. On very steep slopes, the terraces had to be under 6½ feet (2 m) wide, but lower down they could be wider. Inca engineers planned the building of these terraces at Cusichaca as well as the irrigation and drainage systems. The building work was done by men who were serving their mita. They built terrace walls that followed the hill's shape and held back the soil. The walls also stopped the soil from being washed or blown away. The crop was well fertilized with animal droppings. These terraces are still in use.

arrived. In some parts of the empire, people farmed patches of land at different altitudes so they had a greater variety of products.

Married farmers paid their taxes by working on the lands of the Sapa Inca and the sun-god before sowing their own fields. Once crops were harvested they were kept in state storehouses. Some produce was sent to Cuzco for the Sapa Inca's family or the gods. If the harvest had been poor, the food was shared out among the people.

The farming year

Huaman Poma's calendar showed how closely the great Inca festivals followed the seasons of the year and the farming activities. When plowing began at the end of August, everyone worked together, singing in praise of the Sapa Inca and the sun-god. In the mountains, maize and potatoes were planted before the September rains began. Men dug holes with a foot plow and women threw in the seeds. Once the small maize shoots appeared, boys used their slings to frighten birds and animals away. If the rains were late, llama sacrifices were offered, and people wept tears to try to draw water from the sky.

The maize crop was irrigated in November, and the crops were weeded with hoes in January. By February young potatoes and other root crops were being harvested. The maize ripened in May. It was a month of beautiful flowers, many celebrations, plentiful food, and much happiness, according to Huaman Poma. Before being stored, the maize was dried and the grains were removed. The main potato crop was dug up in June and more young potatoes planted for the next crop. At the end of the farming year, inspectors made sure the irrigation channels were cleaned out, ready for use next year.

TRAVAXO
ZARATARPVMITAN

△ In September the foot plow, or chaqui taclla, was used to dig and break up the ground. It was a long wooden pole with a footrest above the digging point and a handle at the other end. The curved board in the picture was used to scrape earth over the maize seeds.

◁ The Incas used a short hoe with a wide bronze head for weeding and light work. For heavier digging or breaking the ground, they used a heavy stone stuck onto the end of a wooden handle. These tools were well suited to terrace farming, and they are still used in the Andes today.

Up on the high grasslands, where only a few hardy root crops could grow, huge herds of llamas and alpacas grazed. The herds — like the land itself — were divided up among the Sapa Inca, the gods, and the community. Ordinary families were allowed ten animals, which they identified by marks on the beasts' ears. All the animals were kept in community herds. The animal herds of the Colla people, who lived south of Cuzco, were the biggest ones. Spanish historians reported that the Colla never forgave the Incas for taking their llamas and alpacas into the state herds.

The alpacas, with their fine fleece, were shorn regularly. The llama's coarser wool was only suitable for making sacking and ropes, but the animals had other uses. They could carry loads and their meat formed part of the Inca diet.

▽ Shepherds lived with their families in small houses on the cold grassland, or puna. Remains of the stone llama corrals can still be seen in the hills above Cuzco. Although the shepherds were responsible for the state herds, children usually looked after the community's own animals.

Inca homes

Houses in the Inca empire were built of whatever materials people could find: stone, mud, wood, and grass for thatching the roof. A town house would be made of well-fitted stone blocks, and it might have an attic or even a second story. In towns such as Ollantaitambo or Machu Picchu several houses would be built together, facing on to a courtyard.

On the coast, simple houses were made out of a wooden frame with a thatched covering. Some houses were built of mud-dried brick called **adobe** and were painted in bright colors. As there was no rain, a rush mat made a flat roof. The forest people used wood, cane, and thatch to build their homes.

▽ The stone walls of mountain houses were about 6½ feet (2 m) in height. The roof sloped more or less steeply, depending on how much rain fell in the area. Thatch was made of coarse grass called ichu, which was placed on a wooden frame. Often, relatives grouped their houses close together, leaving a space in the middle that was sheltered from the wind. This house at Huilloc is very like an Inca house.

<1 Even in the highlands houses were often made of adobe if there was little stone available. Here on the high plains of Bolivia adobe walls are thatched with ichu grass, which grows in clumps near the houses.

△ Adobe bricks are still widely used today in the Andes. They are made with mud and a little straw. The mixture is then shaped in small wooden frames and left to dry in the sun. If the mixture is wrong, the bricks do not set properly.

Farmers usually lived in small villages near their fields. Although families were big, their houses had only one room. Highland homes were made of rough stones that were held together with mud or of stone foundations and adobe bricks. The houses had no chimneys and no windows, so they were dark and smoky. A thick curtain hung over the doorway to keep out the cold. People, wearing most of their clothes and wrapped in blankets, slept on the dirt floor.

There was no furniture inside the house, but alcoves or niches in the walls made useful shelves. Clothes were hung on stone pegs, while other things, including food, were stored away in big, wide-necked jars. Government inspectors came regularly to make sure houses were kept clean and children were properly cared for.

Much of what we know about ordinary Inca houses comes from Father Cobo's descriptions. There are also many stone house walls still standing. Looking at how people in the Andes use their house space today can tell us something about how people used to live.

△ Jars with wide necks, as well as baskets, were used for storing food and clothing.

Cooking and eating

Maize and potatoes were and still are the basic, or staple, foods of the Andean people. They can be stored and eaten year-round.

Maize was very useful to the Incas. It was eaten toasted and boiled, and both ordinary bread and special cakes could be made with the flour. To grind the maize into flour, it was put on a big flat stone, and a woman rocked a curved stone backward and forward on top of it. Potatoes could be kept for more than a year by alternate freezing and warming in the open air. When they had been dried in this way they were called **chuño**.

Soups and stews were seasoned with herbs, salt, and chili peppers and thickened with a grain called **quinoa**. Father Cobo gave the recipe for a stew known as locro, which was made by mixing potatoes and other vegetables and adding a little meat or fish if there was any. Ordinary people rarely ate meat, apart from the occasional roast guinea pig. Llamas were killed for feasts and sometimes the meat was dried into thin strips.

The royal family also ate all kinds of food, such as the tomatoes, beans, guavas, honey, and avocados that came from the lowlands. Wild guanaco — a distant relation of the llama — deer, and hares were caught in seasonal hunts, and fish was sent to Cuzco for the Inca.

Preparing food

Cooking was a job for women and they usually collected the firewood, too. Trees are scarce in the high valleys and none grow on the grasslands, so dried llama dung was often used as fuel. The stoves were designed so that sticks were fed into an opening and the wood burned very slowly. There were two or three round holes on top of the stove, where cooking pots stood.

△ Big, rounded stones were used to grind maize in Inca times and are often used for other grains nowadays. The Spaniards introduced new crops such as wheat, which is grown in many Andean communities today.

◁ Guinea pigs were allowed to run around on the floor of the house, being fattened up on scraps. Ducks were kept, too. They were eaten on special occasions.

Andean families in the countryside still have a largely vegetarian diet because meat is expensive, but there is always a guinea pig for a fiesta.

In most homes the cooking stove and the sleeping area were at opposite ends. Sometimes the stove was built just outside the house entrance in a small lean-to. When fuel was short, people collected grass or small bushes and the stalks of plants that had been harvested.

△ Cooking pots and kitchen utensils such as bone skewers, bronze knives, and wooden spoons, have been dug up by archaeologists. Some pots were made in a special way so that a fire could be built under them. Cooking pots with lids were usually made out of plain brown pottery and were very simply decorated. Flat plates often had a modeled handle, such as the duck's head on this dish found at Machu Picchu.

People ate twice a day, in the morning and in the late afternoon. Pottery bowls and plates were used by most families, but Inca nobles and officials had silver and gold dishes and drinking mugs that were set out on tablecloths.

If the weather was nice, people sat outside their houses to eat. The women served the meal. For a feast, the community gathered near the chief's home to share their food. Chicha, the beer made from maize, quinoa, or molleberries, was always drunk at feasts. To prepare chicha, women chewed the grain or fruit into pulp and spat it into cloudy water. The mixture was then left to ferment to make beer.

Spinning and weaving

Spanish historians were impressed by the quality and the quantity of weaving they saw in the Inca empire. From the well-preserved weavings found in coastal graves, and from pictures of weavers on early pottery, it is clear that in the Andes there was a tradition of weaving that goes back 2,000 years before the Incas.

Women spent much of their time spinning and weaving. They made clothes and blankets for the family, and one woman from each household had to weave a piece of cloth for the state every year.

Cotton, wool, and the rough fibers of the aloe plant were the raw materials used for weaving. Alpacas provided most of the wool. The finest cloth was made from silky vicuña wool, but vicuñas were wild animals, so their wool was more difficult to obtain.

First the animal's fleece was washed to remove some of the natural oils. Alpacas have gray, brown, black, and white fleece, but the wool was often dyed other colors. Dyes came from plants and animals. For example, lichens produced yellow-brown shades, and red was made from cochineal beetles.

△◁ Inca spinners used a stick which had a forked end. It was called a distaff. A bundle of wool was fixed to the stick, and a thread was formed by pulling a thin piece of wool out of the bundle and twisting it. The thread was fed onto another stick, or spindle, which was weighted at the lower end. The weight was made of pottery. Both fine threads for cumbi cloth and thick ones for blankets were spun in this way. Today weavers on the island of Taquile in Lake Titicaca spin their thread in the same way as those shown by Huaman Poma.

Even the Inca princesses and the Coya sometimes wove clothes for their husbands. Brocades and embroidered fabrics were worn by the royal family. Some of their clothes had lacy borders with geometric designs woven in brilliant colors. The finest weavings, called **cumbi**, were those made of vicuña wool by the chosen women of the acllahuasi. Cieza de León said their work was better than anything he had seen in Spain. They made the Sapa Inca's ceremonial tunics, as well as the special cloth which was burned as an offering to the gods. Professional weavers also wove elaborate cumbi clothing.

Inca storehouses contained enormous piles of weavings at the time of the Spanish conquest. Some was used to supply the army, and fine pieces were often presented as gifts to Inca officials. Weaving was also important in the religious life of the people. Cloth was included in sacrifices on important occasions, when the images of the gods were also draped with beautiful cloaks. When people died they were buried wearing their best clothing.

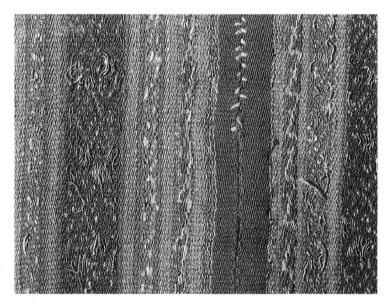

△ The spun thread was woven on a backstrap loom. Two wooden rods held threads, called the warp, lengthwise on the loom. The front end of the loom was tied to a post, while a belt around the weaver's waist held the back one. The crosswise threads, called the weft, were woven through by hand. The weaver used extra rods to vary the pattern of the cloth. Some of the same designs are still woven on backstrap looms today.

◁ Animal, vegetable, and mineral dyes were used to color cloth. For example, leaves from the indigo plant produced a deep blue. The Incas sometimes wove silver or gold thread into special cloth.

An Inca city

Cuzco was the glory of the Inca empire. It was like a holy city. Pachacuti, the ninth Inca, replanned the city so that palaces, temples, and government buildings were grouped in an inner city in the shape of a puma's body. Streams flowed along either side of this section, channeled in stone canals. The holy place, or Huacapata, was a great central city plaza. It was the place where all the public ceremonies took place. Four roads led out of the Huacapata to the four quarters of the empire. Another plaza, the Cusipata, Place of Joy, was used for more festive, less formal, occasions.

The massive palaces of the Sapa Inca, the Coya, and the acllahuasi were built around the Huacapata. Some of these Inca walls still stand, now supporting

▽ Most Inca cities had a large central plaza where people gathered for fiestas or ceremonies. The long plaza at Machu Picchu had the Sapa Inca's palace at one end, and a group of religious buildings, including the sun temple, on the west. Houses were built on the eastern side of the plaza, and terraces and army barracks spread along the mountain slopes. The temple of the moon was placed high up on the loaf-shaped rock and was reached by a steep staircase.

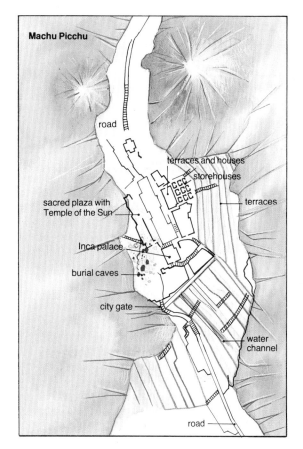

Machu Picchu

road

terraces and houses

storehouses

sacred plaza with Temple of the Sun

terraces

Inca palace

burial caves

city gate

water channel

road

◁ Before entering a city, people had to go through a tollgate such as the one at Rumicolca, south of Cuzco. There they had to say why they were visiting the city, so that officials could keep a check on everyone who entered.

newer buildings. The royal family and all the Inca nobles, as well as priests and officials, lived in the central part of Cuzco. Incas "by privilege" and provincial chiefs occupied the surrounding suburbs and villages. One Spaniard said there were 100,000 houses in the Cuzco Valley.

Like Cuzco, most provincial capitals were both religious and administrative centers. They held many food storehouses and there was often an army barracks. The governor and his staff, as well as the local rulers, or curacas, lived in the city center. Less important people such as craftworkers lived on the city outskirts. Most of the population was scattered in small country villages, visiting the city only on special occasions.

Highland capitals such as Cajamarca , Huanuco, Tomebamba, and Quito were planned with a central plaza similar to that of Cuzco. These cities were essential to the Incas' governing system. Other towns were important for different reasons. Machu Picchu was a religious and agricultural center. Ollantaitambo was an important military position where the Urubamba Valley narrows into a gorge, and another valley route from the eastern forest joins it.

Architects and builders

The Incas produced some of the finest stonework the world has ever seen. To shape each stone their masons used stone hammers and bronze chisels. Throughout the highlands, temples, palaces, fortresses, terraces, and roads still stand as proof of the Inca stonemasons' skill and the huge work force. Earlier Andean civilizations have left monuments, but the Incas precisely fitting stone blocks show greater skill. Father Cobo said it was difficult for anyone who had not seen Inca walls to imagine how excellent they were.

Inca architects used clay models when they were planning buildings. The most important buildings were made of stone, but sometimes adobe bricks were used to form patterned walls.

Near Cuzco, enormous blocks of limestone and granite were quarried. They were probably obtained by driving wedges into the rock face until pieces split away. Thousands of mita workers were needed to haul away the biggest blocks. Some pieces were called tired stones because they were so difficult to move with simple tools such as wooden rollers and ropes.

△ Inca walls often sloped inward, because the biggest, heaviest blocks of stone were placed at the base. Large, irregular shaped blocks might have more than 20 angles to be matched with other stones in a jigsaw pattern. The stones were sanded and polished to fit so perfectly that only a line showed at the joint.

◁ The Incas had not discovered how to build arches, so doorways and windows had stone or wood beams above them. These beams, or lintels, supported the weight of the wall above. Windows and doorway shapes narrowed at the top. The shape is called trapezoid. Sometimes a row of inner alcoves or niches was built for storage spaces. In places, stone pegs can be seen on the end walls. These were used for tying down the thatched roof.

When a high wall was being built, an earth ramp was made so that large, heavy stones could be dragged up it to the topmost sections. Blocks of up to 20 tons in weight could then be levered into place on the wall. The most massive walls of forts or hill terraces were built in this way.

The builders used a style of patterning called **polygonal masonry** for these walls. All shapes and sizes of stones made up the wall. The stones were trimmed with stone hammers, and the edges of the blocks were shaped or beveled so that all the joints were smooth.

Rectangular blocks laid in neat rows were often used for temples and palaces. Although the Spaniards destroyed much of Cuzco and reused the stones, the Inca walls they left have survived earthquakes better than any modern masonry.

△ The steep terraces at the fortress of Ollantaitambo followed hillside contours above the Urubamba River. Many unfinished blocks, hauled from nearby quarries, are still on the site. Some lie by the ridgetop temple.

Crafts and trades

Architects, engineers, and craftworkers had special places in Inca society. They did not have to pay tribute, and they received food, clothing, and materials so that they could work full time.

Craftworkers made luxury goods for Inca rulers, for the priests, and for the state. Their carvings, high quality pottery, cumbi weaving, and silver and gold objects were not made for the ordinary people. Sometimes very skilled workers, for instance, the Chimú metalsmiths of the north coast, were taken to Cuzco from other parts of the empire. They probably taught local workers new techniques, though most craft skills seem to have been passed on through workers' families.

Before the time of the Tahuantinsuyu, the Inca empire, people knew how to use copper, gold, silver, and tin. All these metals were mined during the Inca period by mita laborers. The Spanish historian Pedro Sancho described how gold was mined in narrow tunnels that burrowed 131 feet (40 m) into the ground, although gold was usually obtained from washed river gravel.

Specialists who have studied Inca bronze from Machu Picchu say that it was remarkably pure. The metalworkers knew how to melt tin and copper

▽ A kero, or drinking mug, was usually made of wood or pottery. This kero represents a puma's head, but many were decorated with geometric designs. The royal family drank from gold keros.

◁ This gold tumi knife handle was made by metalworkers on the coast. It was decorated with turquoise and would have been used in religious ceremonies. The Incas also made simpler tumi knives, cast in bronze and hammered along the edge.

△ Inca artisans sculpted small animals, bowls, and human forms in different kinds of stone. Using simple tools, they managed to make highly polished figures like these llamas.

together to make bronze tools or more delicate ornaments.

Metals were smelted inside a clay furnace or **huaira** which had holes in front, allowing the wind to heat up a charcoal fire. Ax heads, knives, and even needles of copper and bronze were made in molds, but precious ceremonial objects of gold and silver were usually hammered into shape by hand. Unfortunately, most of the Incas' fine goldwork was melted down into gold bars by the Spaniards, so that it could be carried away easily and used for other purposes.

Inca pottery was made by shaping coils of clay on top of each other. The pots were painted with liquid clay in white, purple, red, or black and then hardened over open fires. Geometric patterns, especially diamonds, triangles, and parallel lines, are common on jugs, plates, and large jars. Styles of decoration varied throughout the empire, but local styles and shapes show that people often tried to copy the best Cuzco ware.

Roads and bridges

Cieza de León said he doubted there was another highway in the world that could compare with the road from Quito to Cuzco. In some places it was smooth and paved, but in others the road cut through rock and over mountain ranges. Everywhere it was kept clean, and there were road markers, storehouses, and lodgings along the way.

The Incas built more than 15,500 miles (25,000 km) of roads, so that armies, officials, and goods could travel quickly and easily through the empire. The main highway along the Andes ran from present-day southern Colombia to the Maule River in Chile. Where the road crossed swampy areas, there were stone causeways. Steps with occasional rest platforms led up precipices and swaying suspension bridges of braided ropes were slung across deep canyons. The coastal highway was wide and straight, though unpaved. It ran parallel to the highland road. Many secondary roads connected the two highways.

△ Inca highways were carefully planned by engineers and inspectors. The roads were built by groups of laborers who were mita workers.

Communications

In order to govern efficiently, Inca rulers had to know what was happening in all parts of the empire. Messengers traveled back and forth between Cuzco and the provincial capitals. These express couriers, or **chasquis,** used a relay system to make sure that messages were sent quickly. They waited for messages and quipus in roadside chasqui posts, and relayed them on to the next post, as fast as they could run. News of a rebellion in the far north could reach the Sapa Inca within six days, according to the chroniclers.

Only those people who were traveling on official business were allowed to use the Inca roads, and they stayed in comfort at government inns, or **tambos**. In each province, people were given the task of looking after the tambos and the chasqui posts.

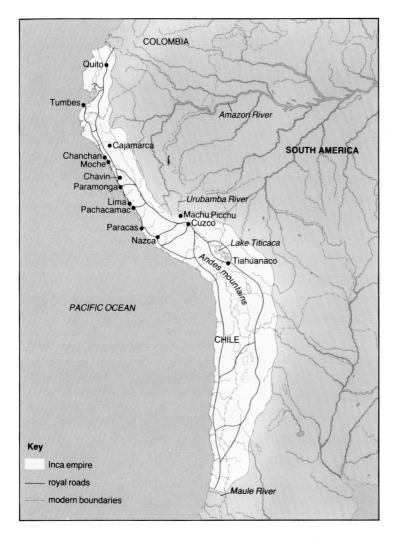

△ Even in the mountains, most roads were fairly straight and wide. They narrowed to about 5 feet (1.5 m) only in very difficult places. On the coast, adobe walls flanked the roads through oases, and tall posts guided travelers on their way in the desert. Some mountain road sections had to be built on stone terraces, with stone barrier walls for safety.

◁ Long suspension bridges were anchored to stone towers on either side of a river gorge. Ropes supported a rush matting footway, and also provided handholds. Mita workers had to remake the bridges once a year in some places. In many places the stone Inca foundations are still used as part of a bridge. This one crosses the Urubamba River between Ollantaitambo and Machu Picchu.

47

Transport and trade

Everyone in the Inca empire traveled on foot, except for members of the royal family, who were carried in litters. There were no horses or wheels until the Spaniards arrived, and llamas could not carry more than about 110 pounds (50 kg). If the load was too heavy, the animal just sat down!

Large herds of llamas took harvest and other tribute goods to Cuzco and they also transported supplies for the army. However, llamas were slow and traveled only about 12½ miles (20 km) in a day, so porters, who could walk faster and carry a bigger load, did much of the work. The porters worked a relay system, like the chasquis.

Archaeologists have found all sorts of objects to show that there was trade between highland and coastal people long before the Inca empire. Some Spanish chroniclers said the Inca state controlled all trade; but others describe local markets and local exchanges between people living in different areas. Money was unknown. Father Cobo pointed out that the Quechua translation of *buy, sell,* and *pay* was "exchange." The royal family themselves organized trading on a large scale. Products exchanged

△ When the Sapa Inca traveled with the Coya they were carried in a litter which was richly decorated with gold and precious stones. Servants, bodyguards, and musicians traveled with them, and there was dancing and singing along the way, according to Huaman Poma.

◁ Eyewitness accounts describe large markets which were held in Cuzco. However, the writers did not explain what goods were exchanged, or who, among the ordinary people, had goods to swap. Jungle products probably included different kinds of peppers, and spices and coloring for cooking, like these on sale in Cuzco market today.

◁ Andean men and women were used to carrying enormous loads on their backs. Sometimes a rope around the forehead helped support the load, and sometimes the pack was wrapped in a cloth which was knotted across the carrier's chest.

included wool, chuño, and llama meat from the mountains for maize, chili, fish, and cotton on the coast. Villagers around Cuzco still swap goods with people in the lower eastern valleys. Today, for example, an alpaca can be exchanged for two sacks of coca leaves.

Some Spanish chroniclers said pebbles or grains of maize were used to add and subtract. People also used a type of rough abacus, which had sets of compartments and counters. The remains of scales for weighing gold and silver have been found on the coast. These scales consisted of a wooden bar with a basket or a pan on each end. The bar hung on a string, and stones served as weights.

△ The Incas traveled more by road than by sea, although they did use big balsa wood rafts with cotton sails for fishing and trading along the coast. The Spaniards also reported that they saw smaller, one-person inflatable rafts. These rafts were made of sealskins filled with air. Highlanders fished in upland lakes from reed boats like the one in the picture.

Weapons and warfare

The Inca army was well disciplined and had excellent communication and supply lines. It was large and moved quickly.

For an important campaign, the provinces sent squadrons of soldiers, who were identified by their own banners. Like the rest of Inca society, the army was highly organized in strict ranks. Each unit of ten warriors served under a local leader. At the next level up there were five bigger units; then there was the captain, who was responsible for 2,500 warriors; and the commander, for 5,000 soldiers. The commander in chief was the Sapa Inca's brother, or another family member.

Before the army set off from Cuzco there were special ceremonies, including sacrifices and feasting, to ask the gods to bring success. Once on the march, the squadrons camped at tambos and drew their supplies from storehouses. Inca ambassadors usually tried to persuade tribes to join the Inca empire peacefully, but often the empire was enlarged only after battle and conquest.

The Incas had more soldiers and better weapons than neighboring peoples. They were also skilled in

△ Soldiers often wore quilted tunics and shields made of wood and cotton on their backs. Another wooden shield on the arm and helmets of quilted cotton or wood provided extra protection against enemy blows. Officers wore richer uniforms and easily recognizable plumed helmets. However, Inca armor was of little use against sharp Spanish swords.

◁ An Inca soldier's main weapons were a sling, a fire-hardened spear, and a star-headed mace (*top left*). Squadrons from other provinces used bows and arrows, blowguns, and stones tied together by cords, which were thrown to entangle the enemy's legs.

planning their attacks. Often they would strike at a time or place which was not expected. When the people were surprised by an attack it was easier to conquer them.

At the start of a battle, slings were used to hurl large stones at the enemy. Then as the armies got closer, troops fired arrows and darts. In hand-to-hand fighting, warriors fought with battle-axes, spears, and star-headed maces. They defended themselves with wooden shields. Trumpets, flutes, and tambourines were played loudly to encourage the Inca soldiers, who also shouted furiously to terrify the enemy. If the Sapa Inca was with the army, he stayed in his litter, with his personal bodyguard to protect him.

Highlanders often retreated into hill forts when they were attacked. This meant that a long siege would follow, while the Inca army tried to starve them out. After an important victory the Incas took prisoners back to Cuzco with them. There were tremendous celebrations, at which soldiers who had shown great bravery in the campaign were well rewarded.

▽ The great fortress of Sacsahuaman overlooked the city of Cuzco. Historians think that the fortress was probably begun by Pachacuti, the ninth Sapa Inca and continued by the Topa Inca. Some Inca fortresses were specially built to protect important towns. They not only had to be in a strong defensive position, but they also had to have room to shelter people from the surrounding area, and they needed plentiful supplies of food and water. The remains of smaller forts, which housed army units in newly conquered territories, can be seen on the far northern and southern frontiers of the Tahuantinsuyu.

The last Incas

When the historians described what life was like in the Inca empire, they usually wrote about the last 100 years. Pachacuti began to rule at this time, so his is the period we know most about. Not only did this ninth Sapa Inca extend the empire's boundaries, he also built a great many roads, forts, and cities in the new territories. He made new laws and reformed the army.

Topa Inca and Huayna Capac, the tenth and eleventh Sapa Incas, tried to combine further conquests with strong government. They made sure that even the most distant chiefdoms sent in their tribute to the Sapa Inca and worshiped Inca gods. However, as the empire grew, it became more difficult to control. Both these rulers were threatened by local rebellions which they had to put down. Many Inca mitimaes, or settlers, were sent to conquered peoples to try to help them live the Inca way of life. When the Spaniards came they said there were more settlers than any other people in many areas of the empire.

During the reign of Huayna Capac there were strange unsettling events, including earthquakes, tidal waves, and gloomy prophecies. One night the

◁ Many fortresses were built in the northern provinces to house Inca soldiers. Ingapirca, north of Tomebamba, dominated the territory of the troublesome Canari tribes. It was probably a sun temple and astronomical observatory, too.

◁ Large rectangular storehouses with plenty of windows for ventilation were built on steep slopes above the Urubamba Valley. Army supplies, food, and clothing were stored near towns and provincial capitals as part of the Incas' efficient administration system.

moon had three halos, which the priests interpreted as meaning blood, ruin, and the end of the empire. While Huayna Capac was in the north, news reached him of the arrival of strange, bearded white men on the Pacific coast. Soon afterward, a new and terrible illness struck the people. It was probably smallpox brought by the Spaniards. Huayna Capac himself, his eldest son, and thousands of the Inca people died in this epidemic.

War between brothers

Huayna Capac had not chosen an heir before he died. His son Huáscar, who was in Cuzco, was crowned, but the long rivalry between Huáscar and his half brother, Atahuallpa, now resulted in civil war. Atahuallpa, with his father's northern army, defeated Huáscar and later had him killed. Atahuallpa was with the army in Cajamarca when the Spanish conquerors arrived in force.

△ Huayna Capac spent a lot of time in the northern provinces of the empire. He built a magnificent palace at Tomebamba, south of Quito, and he improved the roads between Quito and Cuzco. As a ruler he earned great respect and devotion for his sense of justice, according to one chronicler.

The Spanish conquistadors

The Spaniards began to explore the Pacific coast of South America in 1522. Francisco Pizarro, who had arrived in these new lands 20 years earlier, was already a rich and important citizen of Panama, in the north of the continent. Pizarro's first expedition south from Panama met a large raft carrying silver and gold ornaments, emeralds, and rich cloth embroidered with patterns of colored animals. For the Spaniards, this was the first evidence of a great civilization, but they soon found much more to excite them along the coast of what is now Peru. Pizarro gained Spanish royal support for another voyage of discovery, and he was named governor of Peru.

During 1531 and 1532 Pizarro and his small army of adventurers explored the coast, finding some towns in ruins as a result of the civil war between Huáscar and Atahuallpa. An envoy sent by Atahuallpa visited the Spanish camp and invited the explorers to visit Cajamarca. In November 1532, Pizarro led about 160 horsemen and foot soldiers into the Andes. Marching nervously up canyons to the high passes, the Spaniards were constantly overlooked by forts. Pizarro's half brother Hernando wrote that the Incas could easily have overcome them on this march. On

△ As the Spaniards climbed toward Cajamarca through the jagged mountains, messengers went back and forth between Atahuallpa and Pizarro. One Inca messenger was asked what kind of people these Christians were, and what arms they carried. He reported that they were brave warriors who rode animals that traveled like the wind. The soldiers on horses carried long spears which killed anyone who got in the way. The foot soldiers had very sharp swords which could cut a man in half, and they could also throw balls of fire, killing many people.

◁ Francisco de Jerez said that the town of Cajamarca lay on a hillside above flat, cultivated land in the valley bottom. Today the city surrounds the old hilltop site.

November 15, 1532, the Spaniards came out of the mountain passes and looked down on the rich farmland of Cajamarca Valley. The tents of the enormous Inca army were spread out on the other side of Cajamarca City.

Among Pizarro's troops were captains such as Diego de Almagro, Hernando de Soto, and Sebastián de Benalcázar, all of whom played important parts in the Spanish conquest. They were ambitious, determined men who were there to find glory and gold, to expand the Spanish empire, and to convert people they thought of as savages into Christians.

Also with Pizarro were the men who wrote the few eyewitness accounts of the last days of the Inca empire. They included Francisco de Jerez, the leader's secretary.

△ Atahuallpa was not in Cajamarca. Pizarro had to send one of his captains to a nearby bathhouse to find the Sapa Inca. The remains of the hot baths can still be seen today.

Atahuallpa's welcome

Atahuallpa, surrounded by his chiefs and women, received the Spanish captain in a small house near the baths. He did not believe that such a small Spanish force could be any danger to him, so he agreed to meet Francisco Pizarro in Cajamarca square the next day.

Before the meeting Spanish soldiers hid in buildings around the plaza. Atahuallpa, richly dressed and wearing an emerald collar, arrived in his litter with about 5,000 men. He said later that he thought the Spaniards were hiding from him in fear. Then a Spanish priest came out to talk to Atahuallpa. The priest spoke of Christianity and showed the Sapa Inca a book. Atahuallpa leafed through the pages, then dropped the book. Suddenly, the Spaniards attacked, firing cannon, and charging their horses into the plaza. Atahuallpa's nobles were slaughtered, and in the chaos he himself was captured. In panic, the unarmed Inca soldiers tried to escape, but the Spaniards went on killing until thousands lay dead.

△ Atahuallpa (*above*) was interested and impressed when he saw the Spaniards' horses for the first time. The horses gave the conquistadors an enormous advantage in battle and allowed them to move around the country fast. The Spaniards themselves, with their beards and armor and sharp iron swords, were awe-inspiring, too. Yet the writer Pedro Pizarro was still convinced that if the Inca empire had not been weakened by civil war, the Spaniards would not have conquered it with less than a thousand men.

◁ Hardly any of the Incas' fine goldwork survived the Spanish conquest. At Cajamarca more than 12 tons of gold objects, including figures, jewelry, and even a fountain, were melted in furnaces. Pizarro sent a fifth of the treasure back to the Spanish monarchs. The rest of the gold was divided up among the conquerors. This gold mask representing the sun is similar to Inca work.

Hardly believing their success, the Spaniards rode into the Inca army camp the next day and took all the gold they could find. Atahuallpa quickly realized how much the Spanish soldiers hungered for gold, and he offered to fill a room with gold objects in exchange for his freedom. Pizarro agreed, allowing Atahuallpa to think that he would soon be free to return to Cuzco to rule his empire.

At last, after more than seven months, Pizarro started melting down the treasure which had been collected. At that point, Atahuallpa finally understood that his captors might not keep their word.

The Inca was right. The Spaniards accused him of sending for an army and sentenced him to death. Atahuallpa was christened just before he was strangled in Cajamarca square. His murder left the Incas in confusion, without a leader, and the Spaniards were then ready to press on to Cuzco, the heart of the Tahuantinsuyu.

△ The Spaniards decided to crown Manco Inca, one of Huayna Capac's sons, as Sapa Inca because they thought he was friendly toward them. However, instead of allowing the Spaniards to rule through him, Manco Inca turned against the invaders. He tried to recapture Cuzco. While Cuzco was under siege, Manco Inca withdrew to the fortress of Ollantaitambo (*above*). The Spaniards were horrified when they saw the fort's superb position. By this time the Incas had some Spanish weapons and even a few horses, and they attacked so fiercely that the Spaniards had to retreat to Cuzco. Manco Inca decided he would be safer in the forests of Vilcabamba. However, he did not escape. He, too, was murdered by the Spaniards.

Spanish rule

For 40 years Inca rebels tried to keep their government and religion alive in the forest-covered mountains of Vilcabamba. Tupac Amaru, the last Sapa Inca, was unfairly put on trial and executed by the Spaniards, after which the Inca family could no longer fight the conquistadors.

The Spaniards, unlike the Incas, did not pay any attention to the customs and traditions of the people they conquered. They introduced entirely new ideas, such as money, slavery, and Roman Catholicism to the Inca empire. They also carried new European diseases, including smallpox, measles, and typhus. The population of the Tahuantinsuyu probably fell from over six million to less than two million in the 50 years after the Spaniards arrived. The Inca empire was shattered by the effects of war, disease, and the Spanish conquest.

The Spaniards not only took over the lands farmed for the Sapa Inca and the sun-god, they also forced people to pay impossibly high taxes and to work a mita which amounted to slavery in the new Potosí silver mines. Even Spanish officials wrote in shame of the hardship and poverty caused to the people by their government.

△ Inca, Catholic, and other religious beliefs have mixed together in the Andes, and it is often difficult to tell exactly who or what people are worshiping. Many Catholic festivals coincide with Inca ones.

◁ In many parts of Peru, Bolivia, and Ecuador, llama herds are still kept on the high grasslands and used to carry loads. This one is on a road south of Quito.

◁ One of Atahuallpa's great generals, Ruminahui, fought in the northern part of the empire. He is honored by a statue outside the university in Quito, and Ecuadorans are proud of his resistance to the Spanish conquerors.

The Inca heritage

Many Andean traditions did survive the destruction of the Tahuantinsuyu. At least six million people speak Quechua in modern Peru, Ecuador, and Bolivia, and in some communities the food, the farming terraces, and the houses of today would be recognizable to the Incas. Village festivals are often held at the same time as they used to be in Inca days, though Catholic saints are paraded now around the square. Ancient superstitions live on, and huacas still receive their offerings in the countryside.

Some people are working to preserve this Inca heritage, and would even like to have a new Tahuantinsuyu. The evidence of a great civilization is still visible, and there remains much more to be found out about the Incas.

△ One bridge system probably used by the Incas to cross wide rivers consisted of a basket or platform slung on a thick rope. The person sat down and was pulled across with other ropes.

Time line

B.C.

12,000 on — Nomadic people were living in the Andes, surviving by hunting animals

2000 — Farming and pottery making already well established on the Pacific coast of South America

900 – 200 — Chavín de Huantar, one of the first important religious centers, influenced many tribes

A.D.

200 – 500 — The Nazca state flourished on the south coast of Peru

200 – 600 — The Mochica state grew on the north coast of Peru

500 – 1000 — The Tiahuanaco ceremonial center was built up and influenced a large area, far beyond Lake Titicaca

600 – 1000 — The Huari empire controlled much of the southern highlands of Peru, then collapsed

1200 — The Incas were established in the Cuzco Valley

1300 — The Chimú state was growing strong on the north coast of Peru

1438 — Pachacuti defeated the Chanca tribe, and was crowned as ninth Inca ruler

1492 — Christopher Columbus landed in the West Indies

1513 — The Spaniards reached the Pacific Ocean at Panama

1522 — The Spaniards began to explore the west, or Pacific, coast of South America

1525 — The eleventh Sapa Inca, Huayna Capac, and his son died in an epidemic (probably smallpox). Civil war broke out between Huáscar and his halfbrother Atahuallpa. Huáscar was defeated

1532 — November. Francisco Pizarro marched into the Andes, captured Atahuallpa, and slaughtered his nobles

1533 — July. Atahuallpa was executed in Cajamarca square and his empire fell into chaos without its leader

1533 — November. Francisco Pizarro entered Cuzco, the heart of the Inca empire

1533 — December. Manco Inca crowned by the Spaniards

1533 – 1534 — Pedro Sancho de la Hoz and Francisco de Jerez wrote accounts of the first years of the Spanish conquest of the Incas

1536 — Manco Inca's forces almost recaptured Cuzco

1541 — Francisco Pizarro was murdered by a rival conquistador's supporters

1544 — Manco Inca was murdered in Vilcabamba

1553 — 1554 Pedro Cieza de León
published his chronicles of
Peru and the Spanish
conquest, with many details of
Inca life

1571   Pedro Pizarro, a relation of
Francisco Pizarro, published
his account of the first years of
the Spanish conquest of the
Incas

1572   Tupac Amaru, the last Inca to
rule, was executed by the
Spaniards

1580 — 1620 Felipe Huaman Poma de Ayala
wrote his picture history of the
Incas and the Spanish
conquest

1590 — 1611 Friar Martín de Murua wrote
and illustrated a study of the
Incas

1609 — 1617 Garcilaso de la Vega
published his Royal
Commentaries on the Incas

1653   Father Bernabé Cobo
published a history of the New
World, with detailed accounts
of Inca customs

1911   Hiram Bingham found the lost
city of Machu Picchu

Glossary

aclla: a young girl or chosen woman who usually served the Inca religion or the Sapa Inca

acllahuasi: a house or convent where the women chosen to serve in the temple lived

adobe: mud bricks dried in the sun, or a mud wall

alpaca: South American animal related to the camel, which is bred for its long woolly hair

amulet: anything which was carried or worn to bring good luck or for protection

apacita: a pile of stones beside a road or track, built up by people who added to it stone by stone. Each stone meant a prayer for a safe journey

apu: a governor in charge of one of the four quarters of the Sapa Inca's empire, or a lord

archaeologist: Someone who studies old civilizations or history, usually by uncovering buried buildings and objects

ayllu: a family or community group in the Andes

camayoc: a local leader or headman

ceques: imaginary lines which led out from the city of Cuzco. Holy places were grouped along these lines

chasqui: a runner or courier who carried messages all over the Inca empire using a relay system

chronicler: a person who writes about historical events as they are happening

chuño: preserved or dried potatoes eaten by the Incas

Coya: the queen. The wife of the Sapa Inca who was also one of his sisters

cumbi: the finest pieces of woven cloth, made by the temple women using the wool of the vicuña

curaca: a local chief ruling in the provinces of the Inca empire, with some special privileges

excavate: to uncover something by digging

huaca: a place or object of Inca worship

huaira: a clay oven or furnace used by the Incas to melt down the metal for making weapons and tools

huarochico: the ceremony at which an Inca boy received his adult name

oracle: the place where the Incas believed their gods could be contacted. Also a person who was able to contact the gods

polygonal masonry: a style of building, used by the Incas, that uses stone blocks with more than four sides

Quechua: the main language spoken in the Inca empire, and the name of a tribe living in the empire

quicochico: the ceremony when an Inca girl was given her adult name

quinoa: type of grain grown by the Incas, which they used in cooking soups and stews

quipu: strings with knots in them, used by the Incas for keeping records instead of writing

quipucamayoc: a keeper of quipus, or records, in the Inca empire

solar: to do with the sun

suyu: a quarter of the Inca empire

Tahuantinsuyu: the Inca empire, which was divided into four quarters, or suyus

tambo: a resting place or inn for the government officials who were allowed to use the Inca roads

tribute: payment made to the Sapa Inca in the form of goods, or work. Tributes paid for the government of the Inca empire

uillac uma: the Inca's chief priest. He was a member of the royal family and was a very important person in the Inca empire

vicuña: a South American animal related to the camel, which is bred for its fine, silky wool

yanacona: the people who served Inca royalty and the sun

Index